Table of Contents

Front cover design provided by canva

To my boys, always and forever my sunshine.

Chapter 1: What is non-verbal autism?

Five years ago, I gave birth to my third son, Tiggs. He is such a happy, smiley, and energetic boy. Having already raised two children, I felt pretty confident (well, mostly) about navigating the early years of parenting again. After all, I'd done it twice before, so what could be so different this time? Looking back now, I realize I had no idea of the challenges that lay ahead for our family.

By the time Tiggs was about two, I began to notice some differences. He only spoke a few words, made minimal eye contact, didn't respond to his name, and had very limited interaction with family members, let alone anyone outside the family. There were other signs of autism too, but because this was during COVID-19, we chalked it up to the lockdown and the lack of interaction with other children. We had little experience and even less understanding of autism, especially non-verbal autism.

In this book, I use the term non-verbal, though I understand that other terms like non-speaking and pre-verbal may be preferred by some within the autistic community. Currently, non-verbal is the term that feels right for us, but that may change when Tiggs is able to express his own preference.

Tiggs was finally diagnosed with autism around the age of three. By that time, he was still non-verbal, maintained minimal eye contact, and was showing some challenging behaviours. I quickly realized that my usual parenting methods weren't working; Tiggs didn't seem to respond to verbal instructions the way my other kids had. It became clear that he was more of a visual and interactive learner, so I knew I needed to adjust my approach.

I searched for a quick-read book that offered practical strategies to help with the day-to-day challenges of raising a non-verbal autistic child, something that could make our everyday life a little less stressful. After several years of navigating this journey, I decided to write this book from a parent's perspective. My aim is to share my experiences and the lessons I've learned along the way. This book is intended as a quick ideas guide for parents who, like me, are just beginning their journey into the unique world of raising a non-verbal autistic child.

I wish you and your child the very best on your journey, and I hope you find this book helpful.

What is non-verbal Autism?

Non-verbal autism is a subtype of autism spectrum condition (ASC) where people don't develop spoken language in the usual way. Non-verbal autism is not a specific condition, individuals are diagnosed with autism and being non-verbal is sometimes a characteristic of their autism. Autism is a spectrum condition. meaning that it affects people in different ways and varying degrees. Being non-verbal can be tough because it makes communicating basic needs, feelings, or thoughts much harder. Non-verbal autism does not mean, in all cases, that the child cannot understand words or speech or does not interact. Being non-verbal doesn't define an individual's understanding, intelligence or potential. Delays in language development are common in autistic individuals, and up to 30% of autistic people are non-speaking – completely, temporarily, or in certain contexts (UK Parliament postnote, 2020). People with non-verbal autism might not talk or may use just a few words. Instead, they might rely on gestures, facial expressions, or sounds to be understood.

Some signs of non-verbal autism include:

1. **Lack of Speech Development**:
    - Delayed or minimal speech.
    - May use few or no words, or words might be used and then not used again (regression).

2. **Challenges with Social Interaction**:
    - Limited eye contact.
    - Reduced social smiling.
    - Difficulty understanding social cues.
    - Preference for solitary activities.

3. **Nonverbal Communication Challenges**:
    - Limited use of gestures (e.g., pointing, waving).
    - May repeat words or phrases (echolalia).
    - Difficulty with joint attention (e.g., following a gaze).

4. **Repetitive Behaviors and Restricted Interests**:
    - Repetitive movements (e.g., hand-flapping).
    - Intense focus on specific objects or routines.

o   Distress from changes in routine.

5. **Sensory Sensitivities**:

   o   Overreacts or underreacts to sensory input (e.g., sounds, lights).

   o   May have strong preferences or aversions to certain textures or environments.

6. **Difficulty Understanding Language**:

   o   Limited response to name.

   o   Difficulty following simple instructions.

7. **Regression of Skills**:

   o   Loss of previously acquired language or social skills.

8. **Unusual Play Patterns**:

   o   Lack of pretend play.

   o   Repetitive or ritualistic play activities.

9. **Emotional and Behavioral Differences**:

   o   Frequent meltdowns or shutdowns when overwhelmed.

   o   Difficulty regulating emotions.

10. **Delayed or Atypical Developmental Milestones**:

   o   Possible delays in motor skills or coordination.

The reasons behind non-verbal autism are complex and not fully understood yet. However, various studies have pointed to genetic, neurological, and environmental factors. Recent research has linked numerous gene mutations with autism. Both inherited and spontaneous mutations contribute, suggesting autism arises from multiple genetic and environmental factors combined. The genetic predisposition, in combination with some environmental factors, affects how the brain grows and develops. Which creates differences in brain structure and connectivity, specifically regions in communication, sensory processing, and social behaviour. For example, differences in brain areas like the corpus callosum, which links both sides of the brain and the amygdala, which is the area concerned with emotional regulation, have been identified in individuals with autism. These brain differences help explain why communication and emotional regulation can be challenging for non-verbal individuals.

Even though they might not speak, individuals with non-verbal autism can have a wide range of cognitive abilities. Autism is a spectrum, so some might have significant learning disabilities, but others could have average or high intelligence. You just need to find the communication approach that best works for them, communication is key!

What works?

Non-verbal autistic children often learn best through approaches that cater to their unique communication styles and sensory needs. Visual aids, such as pictures, symbols, and videos, are particularly effective because they provide clear, concrete representations of concepts.

Routine and structure also play a crucial role. Consistent schedules and repetitive activities help non-verbal autistic children feel secure, making it easier for them to absorb new information. Hands-on, sensory-based learning experiences are another key component, as many non-verbal autistic children are highly responsive to sensory-based learning.

Individualised learning plans, tailored to each child's strengths and challenges, are essential. Working at their own pace, with frequent movement breaks and positive reinforcement, allows them to thrive. Collaboration between educators, therapists, and parents ensures that learning is holistic, addressing not only academic skills but also communication, social interaction, and emotional regulation.

Recognising signs of autism early can lead to timely evaluation and intervention, which can significantly improve outcomes for children with non-verbal autism. If you notice signs of autism, consulting medical professionals is important for proper diagnosis and support.

The Diagnosis Procedure

Diagnosing autism is a thorough process that involves several steps to ensure an accurate assessment. It usually starts when parents or caregivers notice that their child is developing differently from their peers. They might see signs like delayed speech, limited eye contact, or repetitive behaviours. These concerns are typically raised with a General Practitioner (GP), health visitor, or paediatrician, depending on where you live. The healthcare provider will begin by assessing the child's development to see if further evaluation is needed.

In our case, we became concerned about how much Tiggs understood. He showed little eye contact and had repetitive behaviours. In the UK, health visitors regularly check children's development, and ours conducted age-related ASQ questionnaires. One questionnaire was a general assessment based on his age, while the other focused on his social and emotional development. The results showed some concerns, particularly with his social and emotional scores. This led to a referral to the child development centre for a more detailed assessment. At this point, our health visitor also mentioned that Tiggs had global developmental delay, meaning he was significantly behind in several areas, like fine motor skills, problem-solving, and communication. This confirmed to us that he had significant developmental delays. Tiggs' nursery also supported us, noting that they saw signs of autism in his behaviour.

If a doctor or health visitor suspects autism, they will refer the child to a specialist for a more comprehensive assessment. Having support from a school or nursery can be very helpful in this process. Depending on where you live, the referral could be to a developmental paediatrician, child psychiatrist or psychologist, or neurologist. Often, a multidisciplinary team of professionals—including speech and language therapists, psychologists, doctors, and occupational therapists—will carry out a thorough assessment. Waiting times for these referrals can vary widely. Some families may wait several months, while others might face years of waiting due to high demand. This also depends on whether you have access to private healthcare.

Once referred, the assessment typically involves several appointments where the child's behaviour, communication skills, and social interactions are observed in different settings. Specialists might use standardized tools like the Autism Diagnostic Observation Schedule (ADOS), Autism Diagnostic Interview-Revised (ADI-R), or the Childhood Autism Rating Scale (CARS) to help make the diagnosis. These tools assess various aspects of the child's development, such as social interaction, communication, and play behaviour. Parents are usually interviewed to provide a detailed history of the child's development, which is crucial in making an accurate diagnosis.

The diagnosis isn't based on a single test or observation; it's a cumulative process that considers all the evidence collected from various sources. Once autism is confirmed, the specialists will discuss their findings with the parents, providing a detailed report and recommendations for support and interventions to help the child.

Receiving an autism diagnosis for a child is an emotional experience for parents, often marked by a mix of feelings. The journey leading up to the diagnosis is typically filled with uncertainty, as parents may have noticed differences in their child's development but are unsure of the cause. When the diagnosis is finally made, it can sometimes bring a sense of relief, as it provides an explanation for the behaviours and challenges they have observed. However, this relief is often accompanied by a range of other emotions.

Many parents experience grief as they come to terms with the fact that their child may have lifelong challenges. This grief is sometimes referred to as "mourning the loss of the imagined future" for their child. The dreams and expectations that parents had for their child may need to be adjusted, and this can be a difficult process. The future may seem different to what you had imagined for your child. I still find years later that there are moments that hit me, milestones which I saw with my other children that may pass him by. Give yourself time to adjust your expectations and be kind to yourself. Whilst there are lots of challenges there will also be lots of incredible moments!

Feelings of guilt and self-blame are also common. Parents might question whether they could have done something differently to prevent the condition, even though autism is a neurological difference that is not caused by parenting style or actions.

In addition to grief and guilt, parents may also feel overwhelmed by the prospect of navigating the complex system of support services and therapies available to children with autism. The need to become an advocate for their child, ensuring they receive the appropriate interventions and education, can be daunting. At first, I didn't realise how resilient I would need to become to fight for everything that my son needed. Don't be afraid to advocate for your child and their needs. You know your child and their needs best.

However, often as parents gain more information and connect with support networks, they can move towards acceptance and empowerment. Engaging with other parents who have had similar experiences, joining support groups, and accessing resources can provide much-needed comfort and guidance. Over time, many parents find strength in their role as advocates for their child and take pride in the progress and achievements. One of the groundbreaking moments I had with Tiggs was when he was able to communicate with me, as Tiggs doesn't talk verbally but he does through pictures.

Chapter 2: Communication is key!

Non-verbal autism can be challenging for individuals, parents, and caregivers, but there are some fantastic tools out there to help those who cannot use spoken language to communicate. When it comes to helping non-verbal autistic children communicate, there is not a one-size-fits-all solution. Every child is different, and what works for one might not work for another. Dr Stephen Shore once said, "If you've met one person with autism, you've met one person with autism". That is how diverse the autism spectrum is. But the good news is, there are many communication methods out there, each designed to support children in expressing themselves and connecting with the world around them. Let's dive into some of the most common and effective communication methods for non-verbal autistic children.

PECS

One of the most well-known tools to help non-verbal individuals begin to communicate is the Picture Exchange Communication System (PECS). Dr. Andy Bondy and Lori Frost created this system in the late '80s. It's a type of augmentative and alternative communication (AAC) that uses pictures to help people express themselves and their needs.

To describe it briefly, kids use pictures to communicate their needs, wants, and thoughts. Imagine your child wants a snack – instead of getting frustrated or upset because they can't say it, they can hand you a picture of their favourite snack. You then give them the snack, and they learn that using the picture gets them what they want. It's like learning a new language, but with pictures instead of words.

PECS starts with the basics – just simple exchanges like asking for a favourite food or a toy. Over time, as the child gets more comfortable with this, they can move on to more complex ideas, such as forming sentences with the pictures or expressing emotions. It's all about building up their communication skills step by step. There is a detailed process to follow and training information online at the PECS website: www.pecs.com.

Example PECS book

PECS drawbacks & benefits

It gives non-verbal individuals a way to communicate, which can reduce frustration caused by the inability to express themselves. Using pictures makes understanding and learning easier, fosters social interactions, and promotes independence.

Plus, PECS is flexible. It can be tailored to fit the individual's needs and can be used at home, in school, or out in the community. The system allows for a gradual progression, so individuals can build their communication skills at their own pace.

Using PECS can be wonderful for some autistic individuals, but it does come with some criticism from members of the autistic community because it is based on ABA (Applied Behavour Analysis). ABA is a therapeutic approach that uses the principles of behaviourism to teach and reinforce desired behaviours. The ABA framework can make it feel structured and rigid and may not be suitable for every child. The intense ABA approach can sometimes also be overwhelming for some children. It can also be tough to switch to other communication methods later on. It can also be limiting when there are only a specific set of options that the child can use to communicate. It's all about finding a balance and making sure the approach works best for each individual. PECS is one of the most widely used approaches and I encourage you to research the different communication methods to find the best fit for your child.

Other Awesome Communication Tools

Here are a few other methods that can help:

- **Sign Language**: Some non-verbal children find sign language to be an effective way to communicate, or sign language variants such as Makaton (a version of sign language which uses signs, symbols and elements of speech). Makaton can be good for non-verbal autistic children, and TV programmes (such as Mr Tumble) and Makaton songs can be useful methods of teaching it. The whole family consistently using Makaton to communicate can facilitate a quicker learning speed. Start with a few basic signs to begin with.

- **Communication Apps**: There are tons of apps for tablets and smartphones designed to help with communication. These apps often feature visual symbols, text-to-speech functions, and customizable interfaces. The apps that I have found to be the best are the apps where you can upload your own pictures to make them really personalised, such as the 'Let Me Talk' app, available on Apple devices. I started with snacks and breakfast selection, and moved on to more complicated selections. Below is an example screen of the TV & film section on my son's device. It is completely personalised so he can choose his own TV show or film. You can have different categories in the app for breakfast selections, dinner selections, film & TV, snacks, emotions and much more!

- **Body language:** Sometimes, the most basic forms of communication—gestures and body language—can be effective for us to understand what our child needs. Non-verbal autistic children often naturally develop their own ways of communicating through gestures. For example, my son often takes my hand and guides me if he needs help with something. As parents or caregivers, paying attention to these gestures is important. By recognizing and responding to them, you're reinforcing the child's attempts to communicate, which can build their confidence and encourage more interaction.
- **Object reference:** Object reference is a strategy used with non-verbal autistic individuals, where specific objects are consistently paired with activities or events to

help convey meaning. For example, showing a child your car keys to signal that you are going out in the car. This method helps build understanding for activities and can be useful if you don't have a picture aid to hand.

Speech Therapy

Speech therapy is often a go-to for helping non-verbal autistic children develop communication skills. A speech therapist works with the child to build their ability to produce sounds, understand language, and eventually form words and sentences and communicate. While speech therapy might not lead to verbal communication for every child, it often plays a crucial role in helping them develop other communication methods.

Speech therapists can also incorporate tools like PECS, sign language, or AAC devices into their sessions, making them more personalised to the child's needs. It is about finding the right combination of techniques that work best for the individual child. Our speech therapist played an important role in helping my son communicate. I thoroughly recommend involving a speech and language professional to help on your communication journey.

Communication for your non-verbal child can be tough to navigate, but tools like PECS and other AAC methods make a world of difference. They help non-verbal individuals express themselves, which improves their quality of life and helps them connect with others. With ongoing research and advancements, the future looks bright for even more effective communication solutions.

Chapter 3: Emotional regulation

Managing emotions can be tough for any child, but it's especially tricky for non-verbal children, like those on the autism spectrum. Without the ability to talk about what's going on inside, children can get frustrated, have meltdowns, or completely shut down. There are plenty of tools and strategies out there that can help non-verbal children understand, manage, and express their emotions. Let's dive into some of these, starting with a popular tool called the Zones of Regulation.

What is Emotional Regulation, and Why Is It So Important?

Emotional regulation is all about recognizing, managing, and reacting to emotions in a way that fits the situation. For non-verbal children, this can be a challenge because they can't just say, "I'm upset" or "I'm feeling overwhelmed." Instead, they might show it through their behaviour, for example crying or hitting.

Children often rely on the adults around them to figure out what they're feeling. But when those emotions get misunderstood, it can lead to more stress. That's why teaching emotional regulation is so important—it helps non-verbal children better understand their feelings and cope with them in ways that make life easier for them. Using tools like the zones of regulation means that caregivers can help understand their emotional state and aid them in regulating themselves.

The Zones of Regulation: A Simple Way to Understand Emotions

The Zones of Regulation is a tool created by Leah Kuypers that's used in schools and therapy sessions to help children, especially those with autism, manage their emotions. It breaks down feelings and levels of alertness into four colour-coded "zones," making it easier for children to figure out what's going on inside them.

- **Blue Zone**: This is when a child is feeling low energy—maybe they're sad, tired, or just bored. A kid in the Blue Zone might seem sluggish or uninterested.

- **Green Zone**: This is the sweet spot where everything is balanced. The child is calm, focused, and ready to learn or play. Feelings like happiness, contentment, or relaxation belong here.

- **Yellow Zone**: Things are starting to heat up in the Yellow Zone. The child might feel anxious, excited, or frustrated. They're more alert, but not totally out of control. You might see them being extra fidgety or energetic.

- **Red Zone**: This is when everything is too much. Anger, panic, or total meltdown mode happens in the Red Zone. A child here might be screaming, crying, or even becoming aggressive.

For non-verbal children, the Zones of Regulation can be taught with the help of visuals—like colour charts or apps—that help them point to or show which zone they're in. Over time, they start to understand that each zone means different feelings, and the give them the tools to help them regulate themselves.

Example of zones of regulation

Handy Tools for emotional regulation

There's no one-size-fits-all approach to emotional regulation, especially for non-verbal children. Here are some tools and techniques that can really make a difference:

1. Visual Supports

Visuals are a game-changer for non-verbal children. They help these children understand and communicate their emotions without needing words.

- **Emotion Cards**: These are simple cards with pictures of different emotions like happy, sad, angry, or scared. Children can point to the card that matches how they're feeling.

- **First, then Boards**: This tool shows what the child is feeling right now and what they should do next. For example, "First you're feeling angry, then you take deep breaths."
- **Daily Schedules**: A visual schedule can help reduce anxiety by providing structure. When a child knows what to expect, they're less likely to feel overwhelmed.

2. Sensory Tools

Many non-verbal children have sensory sensitivities, meaning they might be extra sensitive to things like noise, light, or textures. Sensory tools can help them feel more in control.

- **Weighted Blankets and Vests**: These give deep pressure stimulation, which can be really calming for a child who's feeling anxious or upset.
- **Fidget Toys**: These are small objects that a child can manipulate to help focus their energy and calm their mind. Think of things like stress balls, fidget spinners, or even a piece of fabric with different textures.
- **Sensory Corners**: Creating a sensory-friendly space with calming items like soft lights, soothing sounds, and tactile toys can give a child a safe place to retreat when they need to regulate their emotions.
- **Ear defenders**: Ear defenders help autistic children manage sensory overload reducing loud noises and creating a calmer environment.

3. Social Stories

Social stories are short, simple narratives that explain social situations and how to handle them. These can be customised to help non-verbal children manage their emotions in specific scenarios.

- **Custom Stories**: Create stories that focus on emotions, like what to do when you're angry or how to calm down when you're excited. These stories should be easy to understand and visually engaging.

4. Routine and Predictability

Children thrive on routine, especially non-verbal children. Having a consistent daily schedule can make a big difference in how they handle their emotions.

- **Structured Routines**: Stick to a predictable daily routine so your child knows what to expect, this reduces anxiety.

Tricky transitions and time warnings

Transitions can be difficult for children, but when you add in non-verbal communication challenges, they can be even more stressful. Imagine you're super into an activity, and suddenly someone tells you to stop and do something else, at the drop of a hat. It can be frustrating to understand, right? That's why using time-based transition warnings can be great for non-verbal children, especially those on the autism spectrum. Let's break down how to make these transitions smoother and less stressful using some simple time tricks.

What Are Transition Warnings?

Transition warnings are just a heads-up for your child that something is about to change—like going from watching TV to getting ready for bed. Instead of dropping a surprise transition on them, which can lead to meltdowns or resistance, you're giving them time to prepare mentally. It's like saying, "Hey, in a few minutes, we're going to shift activities" instead of, "We're doing this now, like it or not!".

Non-verbal children might not fully grasp the concept of time, but they can understand the idea of something happening soon or next. By using time-based warnings, you're helping them feel more in control. When they know they have a few more minutes to enjoy what they're doing, they're less likely to resist when it's time to move on.

How to Use Time Warnings

Let's get into the nitty-gritty of how you can use time to make transitions easier for Non-verbal children.

Visual Timers: Seeing Is Believing

Visual timers are awesome because they show time passing in a way that's easy to understand. Instead of just hearing "five more minutes" your child can actually see how much time is left.

- **Countdown Timers**: Use a timer that visually shows time running out. There are apps or even physical timers where the coloured part shrinks as time ticks away. It's a super clear signal that the end of an activity is coming up.

- **Timers with Sounds**: If your child responds well to sounds, go for a timer that beeps or chimes when time is up. The combo of visual and auditory cues can be really effective.

Step-By-Step Warnings: A heads up!

Don't just drop a "time's up!" bomb out of nowhere. Ease into it by giving a few warnings as the transition time gets closer. For example:

- "You've got 10 more minutes to play".

- " 5 more minutes left!".

- "2 minutes, then we'll start tidying up".

This helps your child adjust gradually rather than feeling like they're being pulled away from their activity.

One of the things that greatly helped my son to teach saying goodbye and leaving places or items came from a surprising toy, it was a toy post box and letters. We used a toy post box that we would post letters in and say 'bye bye' as we posted the letters. We did this daily over the course of a few weeks, he really enjoyed the process of posting the letter in the box. At the end of those few weeks, he understood that when we say "bye bye" to an item or place it means that we are leaving that place or item. For example, if we are at the swimming pool I tell him we are saying "bye bye" to the swimming pool in five minutes, then two minutes, now we are saying "bye bye" and leaving, he understands what that means and has learned that is the signal that we are leaving. He is calm and prepared to leave because he has time to process it and understands the trigger word to leave.

Visual Aids: Show, Don't Just Tell

Non-verbal children often respond better to visuals than to words alone. So, pair your time warnings with some kind of visual cue.

- **Picture Schedules**: Create a simple picture schedule that shows what they're doing now and what's coming next. It's a great way to visually prepare them for the change.

- **Visual Countdown Charts**: You can make a chart that shows how many minutes are left in the current activity. For each minute or chunk of time, you remove or flip a piece of the chart, so they can literally see time running out.

Practice Transitions: Build Confidence

The more you practice, the easier transitions will get. Start with easy, low stakes transitions at home to build your child's confidence.

- **Routine Practice**: Incorporate transition practice into your daily routine, like moving from one play activity to another. The more familiar they get with the process, the smoother it'll be.

- **Consistency Matters**: Use the same phrases, visuals, and routines every time. This consistency helps your child know what to expect and makes transitions less stressful.

Give a little to get a lot.

Even with all the planning in the world, sometimes transitions are just going to be hard. That's okay! Be flexible and ready to adjust if your child is struggling.

- **Adjust the Timer**: If your child is really into what they're doing, consider giving them an extra minute or two. A little flexibility can go a long way. If my son is in the middle of a line of dinosaurs, I will give him a small amount of extra time to finish his line. I have learned that stopping midway causes far more difficulty than a few extra seconds.

- **Find What Works**: If one method isn't clicking, try something different. Maybe a favourite toy or song can help ease the transition.

- **Giving Choices**: Letting your child make choices within their routine can give them a sense of control, which can help with emotional regulation. You can use PECS cards in the same way to choose toys or activities to do or on your communication device.

Positive Reinforcement and Modeling

Positive reinforcement and modeling positive behaviour can encourage emotional regulation skills and give your child clear examples to follow.

- **Praise and Rewards**: When your child uses a tool or strategy to manage their emotions, celebrate it! This could be through verbal praise, extra playtime, or a small reward.

- **Modeling Calm Behaviour**: Children learn a lot by watching adults. Show them how to stay calm and controlled during stressful situations, and they'll be more likely to do the same.

Combining the Zones of Regulation with Other Tools

The Zones of Regulation works even better when you mix it with other emotional regulation tools. Here's how you can combine them:

- **Zones Chart**: Make a chart with the Zones of Regulation on one side and the tools or strategies that can help on the other. For example, under the Red Zone, you might list "deep breathing," "sensory break," or "quiet time."

- **Toolbox**: Create a 'toolbox' of strategies your child can use when they identify their zone. This might include fidget toys, emotion cards, or a weighted blanket. Encourage your child to pick a tool from the box when they're not in the Green Zone.

- **Daily Routine**: Incorporate the Zones of Regulation into your daily routine. Start the day by finding out what zone your child is in. One day my son will wake up in the green zone, the next he could be yellow.

Helping a non-verbal child learn to regulate their emotions can feel like a big challenge, but with the right tools and strategies, it can be done. By using the Zones of Regulation along with visual supports, sensory tools, social stories, and consistent routines, you can give your child the skills they need to manage their emotions better. It's all about patience, practice, and finding what works best for your child. With time, these strategies can make a big difference in your child's ability to understand and cope with their emotions, leading to a happier and more balanced life. All autistic children are different and unique, but you will find a strategy that works. Sometimes with even the best strategies the child can still become overwhelmed, leading to a meltdown. Sensory overload, difficulty communicating, and changes in routine can trigger intense emotional responses. Meltdowns are not tantrums but a way of expressing distress when the child can't cope, requiring calm, supportive intervention.

Chapter 4: Handling Meltdowns: Tips and Tricks

Understanding meltdowns

So, you've got a non-verbal autistic child who has meltdowns. It can be so tough, right? Meltdowns are intense, and they're different from regular tantrums. They're usually the result of overwhelming sensory input, frustration from communication struggles, or sudden changes in routine. Imagine if you also couldn't express what you needed or wanted – it would be incredibly frustrating! Now, multiply that frustration by ten, and you get a sense of what your child might be feeling during a meltdown. Meltdowns can't always be avoided, sometimes some circumstances are outside of our control, but here is how you can learn to handle the triggers to help your child navigate through these tough moments.

Pre-Meltdown Strategies

Know the Triggers: Keep an eye on what sets off your child's meltdowns, this is so important. Prevention is better than cure. Is it loud noises, bright lights, or sudden changes in plans? Once you know the triggers, you can try to minimise their exposure to them. Make a note after the meltdown happens, so you can see if there is a pattern. Then you can adapt for next time.

Routine, routine, routine: Non-verbal autistic children often thrive on routine. Try to keep a consistent daily schedule. If there's going to be a change, prepare them in advance with visual aids or simple gestures.

Communication Tools: Use tools like PECS (Picture Exchange Communication System), communication apps or the zones of regulation. These can help your child express themselves better and reduce frustration by understanding their wants and needs.

During a Meltdown

Stay Calm: Easier said than done, right? But your child can pick up on your anxiety. Keep your voice steady and your movements slow. This can help create a more calming environment.

Safe Space: Create a safe space where your child can go during a meltdown. It could be a corner of a room with soft pillows, favourite toys, or anything that helps them feel secure.

Sensory Tools: Have sensory tools on hand like noise-cancelling headphones, fidget toys, or weighted blankets. These can help soothe your child when they're feeling overwhelmed.

Avoid Talking Too Much: During a meltdown, your child's brain is on overload. Keep verbal communication to a minimum. Use simple, calming words or just be there quietly.

Post-Meltdown Care

Don't Punish: A meltdown is not a behavioural issue. Punishing your child can increase anxiety and lead to more meltdowns.

Comfort and Reassure: Once your child starts to calm down, offer comfort. This could be through a favourite activity, a gentle hug, or just sitting close by.

Review and Reflect: After things have settled, think about what triggered the meltdown and what could help in future. This can help you prepare better for next time.

Building Long-Term Strategies

Teach Coping Skills: Over time, teach your child coping skills for dealing with their triggers. This could be deep breathing exercises, using a stress ball, or going to their safe space.

Seek Professional Help: If meltdowns are frequent and intense, consider seeking help from a therapist or counsellor who specialises in autism. They can provide tailored strategies and support.

Remember, handling meltdowns is a learning process for both you and your child. Be patient, keep trying different strategies, and celebrate the small victories along the way.

Chapter 5: Toilet training

Toileting can be quite a challenge for children with non-verbal autism, but with patience and the right strategies, it can be done. Let's talk about some practical tips and tools that can make the process smoother for everyone involved.

Understanding the Challenges

Firstly, it's important to understand why toileting can be particularly tricky for children with non-verbal autism. Communication barriers mean they can't easily tell you when they need to go. This is why communication is so key, it's linked to everything. Creating a PECS toilet card can aid with this communication so that the child can signal when they need to go or having a toilet symbol on your communication device. Sensory issues might make the bathroom environment overwhelming, and new routines can be hard to establish. Pinpointing these challenges helps in planning a successful approach.

Getting Started: Signs of Readiness

Before diving into training, look for signs that your child might be ready. This could include staying dry for longer periods, showing discomfort when wet or soiled, or expressing interest in the bathroom routines of others. Even subtle signs can be good indicators.

Start nappy changing your child in the bathroom so they associate this with toileting. It's easier to start during summer months, while children are outside more and less clothes are worn, it's easier to clean up the toileting accidents. Every time they have a toileting accident, show them the PECS card for the toilet take them to the toilet, and change them in the toilet. This will create an association between the process of toileting and the PECS card. Alternatively you may wish to use the sign for toilet or have a picture on your communication device.

Potties that look like mini toilets are available to buy, which may help your child make the link to the normal toilet. Alternatively, your child may prefer to sit straight on the toilet (add a child-sized seat on top). The straight-to-the-toilet method seems to be the preferred method among autistic children.

Watch out for body language indicators that they are going to the toilet, like holding their toileting areas. Children also tend to go at approximately the same times every day. It's worth keeping a record for a few days to see if a pattern emerges. Then you can use that as a guideline for when to take them to the toilet.

We also used a toy doll that, when its belly button was pressed, would simulate going to the toilet. We showed the doll going in the toilet to Tiggs daily as a visual aid to help him understand and connect the concept of using the toilet.

Create a routine around their toilet times

Children with autism often thrive on routines. Start by establishing a consistent toileting schedule. Take them to the bathroom at regular intervals – after meals, before bedtime, and every couple of hours during the day or if you have seen a pattern in the times of day, they are going to take them at those times. Consistency helps them understand when it's time to go and by using visual supports, it provides a guide for what happens when.

Communication Aids

For non-verbal children, communication aids are crucial. Use gestures, signs, or communication devices to help them express when they need to go. If you are using a toilet PECS card or symbol on a communication device, make sure its easily available for them to use.

Visual support can be a game-changer. Use pictures or symbols to create a step-by-step guide for toileting. You can make a visual schedule that shows each step – from pulling down pants to washing hands. Place this guide in the bathroom where they can see it easily.

Make the toilet a positive experience

Celebrate successes, no matter how small. Use positive reinforcement like praise, or a favourite toys or activities when they successfully use the toilet. Highlighting times when they go in the toilet means they are more likely to continue to go in the toilet.

If your child enjoys watching a tablet, books, or songs, these can all make the toilet a more enjoyable place. This can also encourage them to sit for longer periods of time. We had a drawing board for him to sketch while he sat, this encouraged him to sit for longer and made it a more positive experience for him.

Addressing Sensory Issues

The bathroom can be a sensory minefield. Pay attention to things that might be overwhelming, like the sound of flushing, the feel of toilet paper, or the lighting. If the flushing sound is too much, let them leave the room before you flush. Consider using unscented wipes if toilet paper is a problem. Sometimes, small adjustments can make a big difference.

Patience and Persistence

Toileting can take time, and setbacks are normal. Stay patient and persistent. If your child has accidents, stay calm and gently guide them to the bathroom. Consistent, calm reiteration will help them understand the process better over time.

Involving Professionals

Don't hesitate to involve professionals if needed. Occupational therapists, behaviour therapists, and other specialists can offer valuable insights and tailored strategies. They can also help address specific challenges your child might be facing.

Toileting training for children with non-verbal autism is a journey that requires patience, consistency, and a lot of positive support. By creating a routine, using visual supports, addressing sensory issues, and celebrating successes, you can help your child develop this important skill. Remember, every autistic child is different, toileting methods that work for one may not for another. Keep experimenting and stay positive – you'll get there!

Chapter 6: Teeth brushing

Helping a non-verbal autistic child brush their teeth can often be challenging, largely due to sensory issues, but with some patience and creativity, it can definitely be done. Here are some tips to make the process smoother and maybe even a little fun.

Find the right combo

Try different toothbrushes and toothpaste until you find the best (least worst) option.

There are so many different toothbrush options out there, some that are U-shaped, three-sided toothbrushes, flashing and vibrating, and ones that you can connect to play games on your mobile device, the options are incredible. Go through each option and try each one until you find one that your child likes. Do the same with toothpaste, there are flavour-free, foamy options, light fruit options, and varieties of mint. In the end, we went through about 7 toothpaste flavours until we found the very mild strawberry flavour that my son loves. Keep trying, there will be an option that they will like.

Create a Routine:

In this book, the word routine appears a lot, consistency is important for a lot of autistic children. Brush teeth at the same time every day, like after breakfast and before bedtime. A predictable routine can help reduce anxiety and resistance.

Use Visual Supports

1. **Visual Schedules**: Make a visual schedule that shows each step of brushing teeth. You can use pictures or symbols to illustrate steps like getting the toothbrush, putting on toothpaste, brushing, rinsing, and putting everything away. Put this chart somewhere in the bathroom where it's easy to see.

2. **Videos and Apps**: There are lots of videos and apps designed to teach children how to brush their teeth. Watching a short video before brushing or during, can help your child understand what to do. For us, the Duggee teeth-brushing song helped my son understand what was happening. We would play each time it was teeth brushing time. It also helps that it was just over two minutes long, so the right length of time for brushing your teeth. Repetition is essential for understanding.

Turn It into a Game

1. **Timers**: Use a timer, song, or game to make sure they brush for the right amount of time. Many children enjoy the challenge of brushing until the timer goes off or the song ends. It also sets a definitive time period which can help.

2. **Rewards and Praise**: Celebrate the small victories. Offer praise or a small reward after a successful brushing session. I have noticed with my son, that even though he doesn't look at me when he is praised, sometimes he gives a small smile, so even sometimes when you think

it's maybe not been understood, you might be surprised at what is taken in.

Hands-On brushing help

1. **Hand-Over-Hand**: For children who struggle with the mechanics of brushing, the hand-over-hand method can be very effective. If they are happy for you to, gently place your hand over theirs and guide them through the motions. Over time, you can reduce your assistance as they become more comfortable and skilled.

2. **Modeling**: Brush your teeth alongside your child. Children often learn by watching, so seeing you brush your teeth can help them understand what to do. Even if it appears that they are not fully focused on what you are doing, it is surprising what they take in. Make it a family activity to encourage them.

Sensory Considerations

1. **Desensitize Slowly**: This was honestly a game changer for us. If your child has sensory issues, introduce the toothbrush and toothpaste gradually. Let them hold the toothbrush, touch the bristles, and get used to the feel of it in their mouth before you actually start brushing. Try it for a few seconds at a time and gradually lengthen the brushing time. This is really good for children who dislike the sensation of brushing. Gradually my son got used to brushing. It's still challenging but less so than at the start.

2. **Adjust the Environment**: Pay attention to the bathroom environment. Bright lights, loud noises, or strong smells

can be overwhelming. Make the space as calm and comfortable as possible.

Communication Aids

1. **Simple Signs or Gestures**: Teach your child a simple sign or gesture to indicate they're ready to brush their teeth. This helps them feel more in control and makes the process less stressful.

2. **Communication Devices**: If your child uses a communication device, include options for talking about brushing teeth. This can help them express any discomfort or their needs during the process.

Patience and Persistence

1. **Stay Calm**: Toothbrushing can be frustrating for both of you, but staying calm and patient is crucial. If your child senses you're stressed, it can make them more stressed.

2. **Take Breaks**: If things aren't going well, it's okay to take a break and try again later. Forcing the issue can lead to more resistance.

Involve Professionals

Dentists with Experience:

Find a dentist who has experience working with children with autism or SEND. They can offer tips and might have special tools or techniques to help. In our local area, there is a dentist at our hospital that specialises in children with special needs.

Before you take them to the dentist, create a visual schedule to help them understand what will happen at the dentist. With our dentist, we did a ten-minute visit once a month to get him used to the dentist. The dentist didn't even try to look in his mouth the first five times, it was purely to get him used to the environment and process of going to the dentist. After a time, he was used to the process and felt comfortable enough for a quick teeth check. Small steps can lead to big results.

Teaching or helping a non-verbal autistic child to brush their teeth takes time and effort, but with consistency, patience, and the right strategies, it can become a manageable part of your routine. Remember, every child is different, so don't get discouraged if it takes a while to find what works best. Keep experimenting and stay positive - till you find the right mix!.

Chapter 7: Safety

Ensuring the safety of your child is one of the most crucial responsibilities for parents and caregivers. These children often face unique challenges that require extra vigilance, both at home and in the wider world. Non-verbal autism means that these children may not be able to communicate their needs, fears, or discomforts in traditional ways, making it even more important to create a safe and supportive environment for them. Here's a more detailed look at how to keep your child safe, both inside and outside the home.

Inside the Home

Home Security:

Your home should be a sanctuary for your child, a place where they can explore safely. However, because non-verbal autistic children may not understand danger in the same way other children do, securing your home is the first step. Installing locks on doors and windows that are out of reach is essential. Consider adding additional locks on exterior doors (at higher points that can't be reached) or installing childproof locks that require a key or code to open. Door alarms that chime whenever they're opened can give you a critical alert if your child tries to leave the house without your knowledge.

For those moments when you can't be everywhere at once, baby monitors or even security cameras in key areas of the home can provide peace of mind. These tools can help you keep an eye on your child from a distance, ensuring they're safe even if you're in another room.

Safe Zones: Designating a "safe zone" in your home can be helpful. This could be a specific room or a sectioned-off area where your child can go to relax and play without any risk. Remove anything that could be a hazard from this area. This is especially important for those children who like to put inedible objects in their mouths, which is common with non-verbal autistic children. Fill it with toys, sensory items, and other things your child enjoys. Chewable toys such as bracelets, tubes, and necklaces can be bought for autistic children to help redirect the sensory seeking need to safe chewable option. Soft mats on the floor can prevent injuries if your child tends to throw themselves down or move around energetically.

Having a safe zone means that even if you need to step away for a moment, you know your child is in a secure environment. It can also serve as a calming place for your child if they're feeling overwhelmed or anxious.

Visual Aids: Non-verbal children often rely heavily on visual cues to navigate their world, so incorporating visual aids around the house can be a great way to enhance safety. For example, placing stop signs on doors can remind your child not to exit the house without permission. You might also put a picture of a toilet near the bathroom to help them remember where to go if they need to use it.

Visual schedules can be particularly effective, especially if your child thrives on routine. A visual schedule lets your child know what to expect throughout the day, reducing anxiety and the urge to wander off. It can also help them transition from one activity to another without getting upset or overwhelmed.

Outside the Home

Constant Supervision: Supervision is critical when you're outside with your child. Non-verbal autistic children may not respond to their name being called or might suddenly run off if something catches their attention. To keep them safe, always stay close and be vigilant, especially in busy or unfamiliar environments. When possible, having another adult with you can be helpful so that one person can focus solely on your child while the other handles any necessary tasks.

When visiting new places, try to familiarise yourself with the layout. Many locations have a map of the location on the website. I often look at the map on the website and do a mini-risk assessment before visiting. Identify potential hazards and safe spaces where you can take your child if they become overwhelmed. Knowing where the exits are and where the restrooms or quiet areas are located can be incredibly helpful in a pinch. Using special needs pushchairs or reins designed for special needs children (like hobble de hoo reins) can help to keep them safe. I always use the reins near busy roads, or in places there is a risk of danger. My son's sense of danger is extremely limited, and he could easily run into traffic.

Identification: Non-verbal children having some form of identification on them when they're outside the home. This can be an ID bracelet or necklace, a tag sewn into their clothing, or a card they carry in their pocket. The ID should include their name, a brief note explaining that they are non-verbal, and your contact information. You might also include tips for how someone can help your child if they get lost or are found wandering alone.

Familiar Routes: Whenever possible, stick to familiar routes and places when you're out with your child. Non-verbal autistic children often find comfort in routine and familiarity, so taking the same path on walks or visits to the park can help them feel secure. Familiar places are less likely to overwhelm them.

If you're going somewhere new, consider taking a few short visits beforehand to get your child used to the environment. Gradually increasing the time, you spend there can help them acclimate, making the new place less stressful.

GPS Trackers: Technology can be a game-changer when it comes to safety. GPS tracking devices designed for children are available and can be clipped to your child's clothing or shoes. These devices allow you to track your child's location via your smartphone, providing an extra layer of security. If your child tends to wander, a GPS tracker can be an invaluable tool, giving you the ability to quickly locate them if they go missing.

There are various types of trackers on the market, some with additional features like geofencing, which sends an alert if your child leaves a designated area. Others may include a panic button your child can press if they need help, although this feature might not be useful for all non-verbal children.

Teach Safety Skills: While it may take time and patience, teaching your child basic safety skills is essential. Start with simple rules like stopping at the curb before crossing the street, holding hands while walking, or staying within sight in public places. Use sign language, visual aids and repetition to help these lessons stick. Even if you aren't sure that they are displaying understanding, keep going. Keep going, with time and patience it will sink in.

Keeping a non-verbal autistic child safe, both inside and outside the home, requires a combination of vigilance, preparation, and creativity. By securing your home, creating safe zones, and using visual aids, you can create a safe environment where your child can thrive. When outside, constant supervision, familiar routines, identification, and technology like GPS trackers can help keep your child safe in more unpredictable situations. Teaching basic safety skills, tailored to your child's abilities, further enhances their security. With these strategies in place, you can help your child navigate their world safely, allowing them to explore, learn, and grow with confidence.

Chapter 8: Swimming and water safety

Water can be both a source of joy and a significant risk, particularly for autistic children. Many autistic children are drawn to water, fascinated by its sensory properties like the sound, feel, and movement. However, this attraction can lead to dangerous situations, as children on the autism spectrum often have an increased risk of drowning compared to their neurotypical peers. This makes water safety and swimming skills essential for autistic children. I realised early on that my son was entranced with large bodies of water. My son would happily wander off into the sea if he could, he is completely unaware of the danger. With this in mind, we started weekly swimming, so he could learn how to swim.

Why Water Safety is Crucial for Autistic Children

Autistic children can have unique challenges when it comes to understanding and responding to safety cues. Many are non-verbal or have communication difficulties, which can make it harder for them to alert others if they are in danger. Sensory processing issues may also affect how they perceive water, making them more likely to take risks.

Wandering or "elopement" is another concern. Some autistic children may wander off without warning, and bodies of water can be a significant attraction. This is why teaching water safety and swimming skills as early as possible is critical.

Preparing for Swimming Lessons

Before starting swimming lessons, it's important to prepare both the child and the instructor:

Choose the Right Instructor: Find a swim instructor who has experience working with autistic children or is willing to adapt their teaching methods. Specialised swim programs are often available and can offer a more supportive environment.

Communicate the Child's Needs: Ensure that the instructor understands your child's specific needs, including any sensory issues, communication methods, or triggers. The more the instructor knows, the better they can tailor the lessons.

Familiarise the Child with the Environment: Visiting the pool beforehand can help your child become comfortable with the new environment. Show them the changing rooms, where they will enter the water and other areas they will use. Visual aids or social stories can also help prepare them for what to expect.

Use Visual Supports: Visual schedules and cues can be very helpful in explaining the sequence of activities during the swim lesson. This helps the child understand what will happen next and reduces anxiety.

Teaching Swimming Skills

When it comes to teaching swimming, patience and flexibility are key. Each autistic child is unique, so it's important to adapt the lessons to their individual needs.

Start with Water Safety Basics: Begin by teaching basic water safety rules, such as not entering the water without an adult and recognizing safety signs. Reinforce these rules regularly. Repetition leads to understanding.

Focus on Sensory Comfort: Gradually introduce the child to the feel of the water. Start with shallow areas where they can stand and encourage them to explore the sensation of water on their skin. Use toys or games to make this experience positive.

Break Skills into Small Steps: Teaching swimming skills to an autistic child may require breaking down each step into smaller, manageable tasks. For example, rather than immediately teaching how to swim, start with learning to float, kick, and blow bubbles.

Use Repetition and Consistency: Autistic children often benefit from repetition. Consistent practice of the same skills helps reinforce learning. Keep the lessons structured, with predictable routines that the child can rely on.

Encourage Communication: Whether your child uses sign language, zones of regulation or a communication device, encourage them to express how they are feeling during the lesson. This can help the instructor adjust the pace and approach.

Addressing Challenges

1. Managing Sensory Sensitivities:

- Some autistic children may have heightened sensitivity to chlorine, cold water, or the feel of a swimsuit. Consider alternatives like saltwater pools, warmer water, or sensory-friendly swimwear. If your child is uncomfortable, explore different options until you find what works best.

2. Handling Overstimulation:

- Swimming pools can be noisy and busy, which might overwhelm some children. Try to schedule lessons during quieter times or in private pools if possible. Noise-cancelling earplugs or swim caps can help reduce auditory stimuli.

3. Dealing with Fear or Anxiety:

- Fear of water is not uncommon. If your child is anxious, take the process slowly. Use positive reinforcement, such as praise or rewards, to celebrate small successes. Sometimes, watching videos or seeing other children swim can also help reduce fear.

Water safety and swimming are critical skills for autistic children, providing not only protection but also opportunities for growth and enjoyment. With the right preparation, instruction, and support, swimming can become a safe, enjoyable, and beneficial activity for autistic children. Whether it's the joy of splashing in the pool or the sense of accomplishment that comes with learning to swim, the benefits are well worth the effort.

Chapter 9: Bedtime battles: Easing the struggles of sleep

Getting a non-verbal autistic child to sleep better can be like trying to solve a tricky puzzle. Sleep issues in non-verbal autistic children often stem from sensory sensitivities, communication challenges, routine changes, anxiety, co-occurring conditions like ADHD, irregular melatonin production, repetitive behaviours, or medical issues like sleep apnea. These factors can make it difficult for them to fall asleep or stay asleep.

It's a challenge many parents face, and if you're in the thick of it, know you're not alone. Sleep issues are super common among autistic children, especially those who are non-verbal. Whether its trouble falling asleep, staying asleep, or waking up way too early, there's always something to figure out. Here are some strategies and tips to help your little one catch those much-needed Zs.

Establish a Bedtime Routine – and Stick to It!

Routine is everything for autistic kids, especially when they're non-verbal. They thrive on predictability, so having a set bedtime routine can help signal to their brain that it's time to wind down. A good bedtime routine might include a warm bath, some quiet time with a book, or listening to calming music. Consistency is really important. Try to keep it to around 30 minutes to an hour and do it the same way, at the same time, every single night. Over time, this repetitive pattern helps the brain recognize, "Oh, it's sleep time now."

Use Visual Schedules

Since non-verbal kids often rely more on visual cues, a visual bedtime schedule can help them understand the sequence of events leading up to bedtime. Think of it like a picture book that shows them what's next: bath time, pyjamas, brush teeth, story time, and lights out. You can make it fun by using pictures or symbols that they like or understand. Visuals help reduce anxiety because they know what to expect, and there are no surprises.

Create a Calm Sleep Environment

Let's talk about the bedroom. Is it a sleep-friendly zone, or is there too much going on? A lot of non-verbal autistic kids have sensory sensitivities, so their sleep environment needs to be just right. Think about dimming the lights, using blackout curtains or blinds, and keeping noise to a minimum. Remove toys if needed, focus on creating a really calm and restful environment. We went one step further and installed a blackout curtain around the bed, which really helped block out distractions and create a calm environment, focused on sleep.

If your child is sensitive to noise, a white noise machine or a fan can work wonders. Make sure the room isn't too hot or too cold; finding that perfect temperature sweet spot can make all the difference.

Also, consider the bed itself. Are the sheets soft enough? Do they prefer a heavier blanket, or do they kick it off every night? Weighted blankets can be a big help for some kids, providing that pressure touch they crave and helping them feel secure and calm.

Safety and security during the night

If your child wakes frequently and seems to attract danger, a safe sleeper bed could be a great option. These beds are specifically designed for children with autism and other special needs to create a safe and secure sleep environment. With enclosed sides, padded walls, and durable materials, they help prevent injuries, wandering, or falls, ensuring a more restful night. It's a good idea to consult a healthcare professional, like an occupational therapist, to discuss whether a safe sleeper bed suits your child's needs. In some cases, insurance plans or national healthcare systems may cover or partially cover the cost if it's deemed medically necessary. You can also explore charities or organizations that offer grants or funding for families needing specialized equipment.

Melatonin: A Helping Hand, Not a magic fix

Many parents turn to melatonin supplements to help with sleep, and it can be recommended by some paediatricians. Melatonin is a natural hormone that our bodies produce to help regulate sleep-wake cycles. For some kids, a small dose can help them fall asleep faster. But remember, it's not a magic fix. It doesn't always help kids stay asleep through the night. Always consult with a healthcare professional before starting melatonin to figure out the right dosage and ensure it's safe for your child.

Consider Sensory Tools

For non-verbal kids who have sensory processing challenges, certain sensory tools can help calm their bodies down for sleep.

This might include things like a body sock or a weighted blanket.

Limit Screen Time Before Bed

Screens are everywhere these days, and while they can be great for learning and entertainment, they can mess with sleep, especially the blue light from tablets, phones, and TVs. Try to cut off screen time at least an hour before bed. Instead, use this time for low-key activities like reading a book, doing some gentle puzzles, or playing with calming sensory toys. The idea is to help their brains start winding down.

Physical Activity During the Day

A good day leads to a good night. Getting plenty of physical activity during the day can help a child be more tired and ready for sleep at night. Playing outside, jumping on a trampoline, or even a fun walk can help. The key is finding an activity your child enjoys and can safely do. The goal is to get them to burn off some energy, which naturally helps their body wind down later. Not too close to bedtime though, or they could end up becoming more active.

Keep Bedtime Calm – Avoid Late Night Drama

It's important to keep bedtime as calm and positive as possible. If bedtime becomes a battleground, it only creates more stress around sleep. Try to avoid high-energy activities and keep the environment as peaceful as you can. If your child starts to associate bedtime with stress, they're less likely to settle down. Even if things get a bit chaotic, try to stay calm.

Track Sleep Patterns

Keeping a sleep diary can help you spot patterns that you might not otherwise notice. Write down when they fall asleep, how often they wake up, and what their behaviour was like before bed. Over time, you might start to see triggers or certain things that help or hinder their sleep. This can help you make small tweaks and adjustments to improve their sleep over time.

Limit Late Night Snacks and Drinks

While a small, healthy snack before bed can be okay, try to avoid big meals or sugary treats right before bedtime. Sugary or caffeinated drinks will just give them more energy. Keeping food and drink routines predictable helps them know what to expect and reduces the likelihood of midnight wakeups for a snack or a drink.

Use Social Stories for Sleep

Social stories are a great tool to help non-verbal children understand different situations, including bedtime. You can create a simple social story that explains why sleep is important, what happens during sleep, and what their bedtime routine will look like. Use pictures or symbols to make it engaging and easier for them to understand. Reading the same social story every night as part of the bedtime routine can help reinforce what's expected and make the process smoother.

Reach Out for Professional Help When Needed

Sometimes, despite our best efforts, sleep continues to be a battle. If your child is really struggling, don't be afraid to seek professional help. Paediatricians, sleep specialists, occupational therapists, and behavioural therapists can all offer insights and strategies tailored to your child's specific needs. They can help identify any underlying issues, such as anxiety or sensory processing difficulties, that might be affecting their sleep.

Getting a non-verbal autistic child to sleep better is rarely a quick fix. It takes time, patience, and a lot of trial and error. Keep trying different strategies and stay positive, even when things aren't going perfectly. Remember that you're doing an amazing job, and every little step forward is progress.

Navigating sleep with a non-verbal autistic child can be tough, but it's not impossible. It's all about finding the right combination of strategies that work for your child. Routine, visual aids, sensory tools, and a calm, predictable environment can make a world of difference. Remember, you're not alone in this journey—reach out to other parents, join support groups, and lean on the professionals when you need to. Here's to better nights ahead for you and your little one!

To wrap-up

I know firsthand how overwhelming it can be to care for a child with non-verbal autism while constantly trying to meet their needs, often with limited support or information. I wrote this book to provide a bit of help to fellow parents in the same situation, to make the start of your journey a little easier, and to address some of the most common questions you may have.

One book I highly recommend is *The Reason I Jump* by Naoki Higashida. Written from the perspective of a non-verbal autistic author, it offers incredible insight into what life is like for someone who doesn't communicate verbally.

I've kept this guide intentionally short because I know your time is precious and likely stretched thin. If you've made it to the end, thank you so much for reading. I hope you found the information helpful. I would greatly appreciate it if you could leave an Amazon review—whether your feedback is good, bad, or somewhere in between. If there's anything else you'd like me to cover in future books or expand upon, please let me know.

Finally, I wish you and your child all the best on your journey. Parenting a child with non-verbal autism can be tough, but I've found it to be immensely rewarding in ways I never imagined.

Take care,

Ellie O'Brien

References

Causes of Non-verbal Autism

1. **Autism Speaks. (2023).** *What Causes Autism?* Retrieved from autismspeaks.org

2. **Bailey, A., et al. (1995).** *Autism as a strongly genetic disorder: evidence from a British twin study.* Psychological Medicine, 25(1), 63-77.

3. **Casanova, M. F. (2007).** *The neuropathology of autism.* Brain Pathology, 17(4), 422-433.

4. **Feliciano, P., et al. (2019).** Exome sequencing and functional analysis identifies recurrent and novel mutations in autism spectrum disorder. *Science Advances*, 5(9).

5. **Geschwind, D. H. (2011).** *Autism: Many genes, common pathways?* Cell, 135(3), 391-395.

6. **Lord, C. et al. (2018).** *Autism spectrum disorder.* The Lancet, Vol 392, 508–520.

7. **Mundy, P., & Neal, A. R. (2001).** *Neural plasticity, joint attention, and a transactional social-orienting model of autism.* International Review of Research in Mental Retardation, 23, 139-168.

8. **Matelski, L., & Van de Water, J. (2016).** *Risk factors in autism: Thinking outside the brain.* Journal of Autoimmunity, 67, 1-7.

9. **Parliamentary Office of Science and Technology. (2020).** POSTnote 612: Autism. UK Parliament.

Retrieved from
https://researchbriefings.files.parliament.uk/documents/POST-PN-0612/POST-PN-0612.pdf

10. **Sanders, S. J., et al. (2015).** Insights into Autism Spectrum Disorder Genomic Architecture and Biology from 71 Risk Loci. *Neuron*, 87(6), 1215-1233.

11. **Satterstrom, F. K., et al. (2020).** Large-Scale Exome Sequencing Study Implicates Both Developmental and Functional Changes in the Neurobiology of Autism. *Cell*, 180(3), 568-584.

Diagnosis Procedure in the UK

1. **NHS. (2024).** *Autism spectrum disorder (ASD) - Diagnosis. Retrieved from* Autism - NHS (www.nhs.uk)
.

2. **National Autistic Society. (2024).** *Getting an autism diagnosis.* Retrieved from autism.org.uk.

3. **Gillberg, C. (2010).** *The diagnosis of autism and its spectrum.* Dialogues in Clinical Neuroscience, 12(1), 55-63.

4. **Baird, G., et al. (2006).** *Prevalence of disorders of the autism spectrum in a population cohort of children in South Thames: the Special Needs and Autism Project (SNAP).* The Lancet, 368(9531), 210-215.

Parental Emotions

1. **Altiere, M. J., & Von Kluge, S. (2009).** *Searching for acceptance: Challenges encountered while raising a child with autism.* Journal of Intellectual and Developmental Disability, 34(2), 142-152.

2. **Benson, P. R. (2010).** *Coping, distress, and well-being in mothers of children with autism.* Research in Autism Spectrum Disorders, 4(2), 217-228.

3. **Gray, D. E. (2002).** *'Everybody just freezes. Everybody is just embarrassed': Felt and enacted stigma among parents of children with high functioning autism.* Sociology of Health & Illness, 24(6), 734-749.

4. **Hastings, R. P., & Taunt, H. M. (2002).** *Positive perceptions in families of children with developmental disabilities.* American Journal on Mental Retardation, 107(2), 116-127.

5. **O'Brien, M. (2007).** *Ambiguous loss in families of children with autism spectrum disorders.* Family Relations, 56(2), 135-146.

Non-verbal Autism and Safety

1. **Autism Speaks. (2024).** *Safety.* Retrieved from autismspeaks.org

2. **Centre's for Disease Control and Prevention (CDC). (2022).** *Autism Spectrum Disorder (ASD) and Safety.* Retrieved from cdc.gov

3. **Ganz, J. B., et al. (2012).** *Aided Augmentative and Alternative Communication for Individuals With Autism*

Spectrum Disorders. Pediatrics, 130(Supplement 2), S152-S156.

4. **National Autistic Society. (2024).** *Communication and Autism.* Retrieved from autism.org.uk

PECS (Picture Exchange Communication System) for Non-verbal Autistic Individuals

1. **Autism Speaks. (2024).** *What is PECS?* Retrieved from autismspeaks.org

2. **Bondy, A., & Frost, L. (1994).** *The Picture Exchange Communication System.* Focus on Autistic Behavior, 9(3), 1-19.

3. **Charlop-Christy, M. H., Carpenter, M., Le, L., LeBlanc, L. A., & Kellet, K. (2002).** *Using the Picture Exchange Communication System (PECS) with Children with Autism: Assessment of PECS Acquisition, Speech, Social-Communicative Behavior, and Problem Behavior.* Journal of Applied Behavior Analysis, 35(3), 213-231.

4. **Frost, L., & Bondy, A. (2002).** *The Picture Exchange Communication System Training Manual.* Pyramid Educational Consultants, Inc.

5. **Ganz, J. B., et al. (2012).** *Aided Augmentative and Alternative Communication for Individuals With Autism Spectrum Disorders.* Pediatrics, 130(Supplement 2), S152-S156.

6. **National Autistic Society. (2024).** *Communication tools: Picture Exchange Communication System (PECS).* Retrieved from autism.org.uk

Toileting for Non-verbal Autistic Children

1. **Autism Speaks. (2024).** *Toilet Training Guide.* Retrieved from autismspeaks.org

2. **Azrin, N. H., & Foxx, R. M. (1971).** *A rapid method of toilet training the institutionalized retarded.* Journal of Applied Behavior Analysis, 4(2), 89-99.

3. **Dalrymple, N. J., & Ruble, L. A. (1992).** *Toilet training and behaviors of people with autism: Parent views.* Journal of Autism and Developmental Disorders, 22(2), 265-275.

4. **Levy, S. E., & Hyman, S. L. (2005).** *Toilet training in autism spectrum disorders.* Pediatrics, 116(3), e324-e328.

5. **National Autistic Society. (2024).** *Toilet Training.* Retrieved from autism.org.uk

Meltdowns in Non-verbal Autistic Children

1. **Asperger/Autism Network (AANE). (2024).** *Emotional regulation: Advice for families.* Retrieved from aane.org

2. **Autism Research Institute. (2024).** *Meltdowns & calming techniques in Autism.* Retrieved from autism.org

3. **National Autistic Society. (2024).** *Meltdowns.* Retrieved from autism.org.uk

Water Safety and Swimming for Autistic Children

1. **Alaniz, M. L., Rosenberg, S. S., Beard, N. R., & Rosario, E. R. (2017).** *Sensory Processing and Autism Spectrum Disorders: A Review.* Frontiers in Integrative Neuroscience, 11, 49.

2. **Autism Speaks. (2023).** *Swim and water safety.* Retrieved from autismspeaks.org.

3. **Morrongiello, B. A., & Schell, S. L. (2010).** *Child injury: The role of supervision in prevention.* American Journal of Lifestyle Medicine, 4(1), 65-74.

4. **Rogers, L. T. (2000).** *Teaching swimming to children with autism.* Focus on Autism and Other Developmental Disabilities, 15(1), 52-58.

5. **Yilmaz, I., Yanardag, M., Birkan, B., & Bumin, G. (2004).** *Effects of swimming training on physical fitness and water orientation in autism.* Pediatrics International, 46(5), 624-626.

Transition Warnings Using Time for Non-verbal Children

1. **National Autistic Society (2024).** Dealing with change – a guide for all audiences. Retrieved from autism.org.uk.

2. **Greene, R. (2021).** *The explosive child.* Harper paperbacks.

Tools for Emotional Regulation in non-verbal Children (Including the Zones of Regulation)

1. **Kuypers, L. M. (2011)**. *The Zones of Regulation: A Curriculum Designed to Foster Self-Regulation and Emotional Control.* Think Social Publishing, Inc.

2. **Prizant, B. M., & Laurent, A. C. (2011)**. *The SCERTS Model: A Comprehensive Educational Approach for Children with Autism Spectrum Disorders.* Brookes Publishing.

Bedtime battles

1. **Richdale, A. L., & Schreck, K. A. (2009).** "Sleep Problems in Autism Spectrum Disorders: Prevalence, Nature, & Possible Biopsychosocial Aetiologies." *Sleep Medicine Reviews*, 13(6), 403-411.

2. **Malow, B. A., Adkins, K. W., Reynolds, A., Weiss, S. K., Loh, A., Fawkes, D., & Katz, T. (2014).** "Melatonin for Sleep in Children with Autism: A Controlled Trial Examining Dose, Tolerability, and Outcomes." *Journal of Autism and Developmental Disorders*, 44, 2173–2186.

3. **The National Autistic Society. (2024).** *Sleep: a guide for parents of autistic children.* Retrieved from www.autism.org.

4. **Rhoades, R., & McFarland, L. (2020).** "Bedtime Routines and Sleep Patterns in Children with Autism Spectrum Disorders." *Journal of Pediatric Psychology*, 45(8), 950-959.

5. Vriend, J. L., Corkum, P. V., Moon, E. C., & Smith, I. M. (2011). "Behavioral Interventions for Sleep Problems in Children with Autism Spectrum Disorders: Current Findings and Future Directions." *Journal of Pediatric Psychology*, 36(9), 1017-1029.

6. Wiggs, L., & Stores, G. (2004). "Sleep Patterns and Sleep Disorders in Children with Autistic Spectrum Disorders: Insights Using Parental Questionnaires and Sleep Diaries." *Developmental Medicine & Child Neurology*, 46(6), 372-380.

Printed in Great Britain
by Amazon

47436495R00040